I0493423

DSLR Portrait Photography

Simple techniques how to create beautiful pictures
using your DSLR camera

Brad Davis

Copyright © 2015 by Brad Davis.

All rights reserved. No part of this publication may be reproduced, distributed, or transmitted in any form or by any means, including photocopying, recording, or other electronic or mechanical methods, without the prior written permission of the author, except in the case of brief quotations embodied in critical reviews and certain other noncommercial uses permitted by copyright law.

Contents

This book is a guide on how to take good portraits with a DSLR camera. It starts by defining what portrait photography is and what it entails. You will also get to know more about the DSLR camera including how it functions. The book has also explained the different types of portraits which are available.

On reading this book, you will get to know how to adjust the aperture settings so as to take the different kinds of portraits. Close-ups, which an important kind of portrait, are discussed in this book. You will get to understand how to adjust the settings of the DSLR camera so as to ensure that both the eyes and the hair of the subject are in focus.

Group portraits, which involve a group of individuals ready to be photographed are also discussed. You are guided on how to position these individuals in relation to their heights so that no one blocks the other. The camera settings necessary for shooting a group portrait are also discussed.

On reading this book, you will get to know how to blur the background of the subject to ensure a sharp focus on the subject only. You will also know how to brighten portraits taken during the daytime. The common mistakes which photographers make while shooting portraits are discussed and how to avoid them. Shooting atmospheric portraits is also explored as well as how to use flash to eliminate harsh shadows in the image.
The following topics are explored in this book:

Aperture setting for photographing Portraits
Close-up portraits
Group portraits
Portraits with Blurred Background
Brightening day-time portraits
Portrait photography mistakes to avoid
Shooting Atmospheric portraits
Using Flash to eliminate Harsh Shadows
How to hold the camera

Introduction

Portrait photography is a common practice nowadays. One may need to take a photo of a single individual or a group of individuals to express their moods or personalities. However, portrait photography is more challenging as most photographers usually end up getting poor photos. The reason behind this is lack of guides for doing this.

This book will address that issue. Portrait photography needs one to be keen while taking the picture such as on the location of the subject, the settings of the camera and as well as choosing the correct background. Positioning the subject in relation to its background is also a challenge.

While taking portraits, the emphasis should not be on the whole body but on some specific parts. One might also to hide some features associated with individuals such as pimples or wrinkles associated with aged persons. This is challenging and requires much keen while shooting the photo.

The photographer also needs to identify a correct position relative to the subject so as to shoot something good. Background with objects such as trees, posts and other structures should also be avoided for a good looking portrait.

Chapter 1: Definition

Portrait photography is taking photos of an individual or a group of individuals with the intention of displaying of the mood, expression or personality of the subject. Although one has the choice of showing the whole body of individual(s) and the background, the focus is mostly on the face.

DSLR (Digital Single-Lens Reflex camera) is a digital camera. It works by combining the mechanisms and optics of a digital imaging sensor and a single-lens reflex camera. Due to the reflex design, the DSLR camera is totally different from the other kinds of cameras. In this book, we are going to explore the tricks, techniques and secrets necessary for one to take portrait photographs using the DSLR camera.

However, one needs to make proper arrangements with the subject to be photographed. This can be an individual, a family or a group of friends. You can take portraits for professional uses or passports. Artistic and casual portraits can also be taken. The subject needs to remain at ease, make the right pose and also compose the creativity for the image.

One needs to understand how to set the camera so as to adjust how the photo looks to the viewers. However, the different portraits require almost the same camera settings so this shouldn't worry you. What differs is the approach and the techniques to be used.

It is also good for one to understand how to control the amount of light getting into the camera so as to get the right and intended portrait. Otherwise, the portraits produced won't be amazing. The following are some of the portraits:

Candid portrait- this can be taken at any place and at any time. Just carry your camera around with you and people will call you to take them a candid portrait.

Formal portrait- you can use a wall or any solid-colored background. The subject should then be a short distance from it. It is good to review it keenly so as to make sure that you have the right thing. You take the photo severally before getting what intended to have.

Self-portrait- use a tripod stand to put the camera on. The shutter opening should then be delayed until you are ready to take the picture.

Outdoor portrait- be keen on the sun if you need to shoot this portrait. This can be taken very early in the morning or late in the afternoon. At this time, the shadows are soft and the sun gives a golden color. Nothing from the background that should compete or distract the photo.

Mature person's portrait- for this portrait, the aperture of the camera should be set between f/3.5 and f/7.1. With this range, every detail can be focused. If there is a need to eliminate on some lines and wrinkles, then a soft-focus filter s necessary. If the subject has a sagging neck skin, ask them to raise their chin before shooting the photo.

Chapter 2: Aperture setting for photographing Portraits

As we said in the introduction part, one needs to understand the aperture settings very well before beginning to photograph portraits. The aperture needs to be set differently when photographing different portraits. While shooting portraits, the background is of little or no importance and that is why it is recommended you blur it. The focus should be on the subject. However, this should not apply if you are shooting a holiday snapshot.

Rules

If you are taking a photo of a single person, then it is good to use the lowest aperture number that your lens will allow. Good lens can allow it to be f/2.8 which is a small number. For two or three persons, a setting of f/4 is recommended. For more than 3 people, the aperture should be set to f/5.6.

The people should also be sharp. If you set the aperture to a low number such as f/2.8 and then you photograph two or more persons, then the resulting photos won't be sharp. You may get one of the persons in a sharp focus but the rest won't. It is worth to note that if you set the aperture to a high number, then much details will be seen in the photo.

However, this idea is not important in all scenarios while taking portraits. A good example is when photographing an old person. Wrinkles will appear in the photo and they might look multiplied. You will then get a poor portrait. This also applies to taking portraits of people with pimples and other blemishes which are not wanted. The aperture needs to be set to a lower number in these scenarios.

In most portraits, aim at getting sharp eyes but make sure that the other areas are soft. Lower aperture numbers are also good in isolating the subject and blurring the background.

If you adhere to the above discussed aperture settings, then you will never have any issues while photographing portraits.

Chapter 3: Close-Up portraits

This should only be taken if the face of the subject is flawless, otherwise, you will get a poor portrait. However, it is possible to remove some of the errors or unwanted parts during editing.

Setting up the DSLR camera

The DSLR camera needs to be set up well before photographing a close-up portrait. Set the camera into Aperture Priority Mode. An ISO setting of 100 should also be used for this purpose.

If the eyes of the subject are at different distances away from the camera, then an aperture setting of f/7.1 which is small should be used. If you use this aperture setting, the hair will also be prevented from being out of focus. If a dreamy and soft look is needed, then the aperture should be set to f/2.8 which is a small number.

If you want to focus greatly on the eyes of the subject, a single auto-focus point should be used. If you set the focus length to between 100mm to 150mm, then you will get a very good close-up without damaging the features of your subject. To ensure that the image is free of blurring, use image stabilization. It is must that you use a tripod stand for this image. However, if your hand is steady enough, you can avoid this.

Getting the Close-up photo

Now that you have set up the camera, it's time to take the close-up photo. If you need an extreme close-up photo up, soft light is needed. This is why this photo should only be taken near a diffuse window light or during an overcast day. If your area has no overcast weather, identify a shaded area and take the photo from there. Light from a diffused on-camera flash can also be used.

Get the eyes clearly focused. This will make the whole image to look good. If you fail to do this, the whole of the photo will be seen as fuzzy. You can set the aperture to a larger f/stop number if you need to fix eyes which are out of focus. You should then try again. Jewelry can also be used for the purpose of drawing the viewer into the picture.

The tip behind taking this kind of photo is to ask the person to move away from the camera. Let them look at the camera. You should then focus at the eyes and then shoot the photo. You can also ask them to bend the head towards one side and then smile.

Chapter 4: Group Portraits

Unlike in our previous chapter we were taking a photo of an individual person, in this case, we have more than one person. The following are the necessary steps while taking this portrait:

Identify the best location- this is location where the attention of the viewer is not distracted. The background should help draw in the viewer.

Choose the right camera settings- to get the right shallow of depth of field, shoot in Aperture Priority Mode. At the same time, use a larger aperture, that is, a small f/stop number, between f/3.5 and f/5.6.

For a group several rows deep, set the aperture to f/5.6 or to f/6.3. With this, everyone will be kept in focus. The ISO range should then be tuned to between 100 and 400. If the shutter speed is low and the lighting conditions are low, bump it.

 It is worthy to note that, setting the focal length to between 28mm and 100mm makes it able for you to capture both small and large groups. It is not a must for you to use the image stabilization. If taking several shots of the same place, use a tripod stand.

Arrange the group- while arranging the group, no eyes or mouth of anyone should be blocked by any other person. Tall people should be made to stand at the back while short people at the front so as to avoid this issue of blockage. The tallest person in the group should be made to lie on his side on the ground. The others should then kneel behind him.

Prepare to take the photo- it is now time to take the group portrait. To make it unique, stand at a high vantage point, let the group members look up at the camera.

Create focus by pressing on the shutter button halfway. Take the photo. If the group is numerous rows deep, the auto-focus point should be positioned over someone located at the middle. You can then press the shutter button and the group will be focused from the front to the back.

Shoot several photos while keeping the group in place- shoot several photos and observe after each shot. You should stop shooting once you have the one that you intended to have.

In most cases, photographers will stop when everyone in the group is looking at the camera and putting a smile on their face. However, this is not always the case. It is good to ensure that no one has his or her eyes closed before you can say that you have the right portrait. Patience is very good, so shoot until you have the correct portrait.

Chapter 5: Portraits with Blurred Backgrounds

Blurring backgrounds is good as it makes the subject to stand out. This effect can be easily achieved with a DSLR camera. You can adjust your camera to ensure that both the subject and the background are in sharp focus or only the subject is in sharp focus but the background be blurred.

Steps

To take a portrait with a blurred background, kindly follow the steps below:

Set the mode dial of the camera to "A". It is now in Aperture Priority Mode. You can also set the mode dial on canon models "Av".

You can now accentuate this effect by standing back and then zooming in the lens.

Select the smallest available f-number. For kit-lens, this will be f/5.6 after you have zoomed in.

You can then increase the distance in between the subject and the background. This will accentuate the effect further. If you want to shoot the head and the shoulders, the subject should be kept closer to you. They should also be positioned against a distant background.

You can then take the photo. The last step is to reset the camera back to Program Mode or Auto.

If the blurred background is really of importance, then consider purchasing a lens with a bigger aperture. This means that it will have a smaller f-number. Compared to a kit-lens, the blurring effect will be greater with these. Lenses which provide small f-numbers are expensive but they are good for taking perfect portraits.

While purchasing lens, it is good to go for one with an aperture of around f/1.8 or one with a smaller aperture than this. The lens should be of 50mm. These will provide a great blurring effect of the scene and they are also available nearly for each and every DSLR camera. Even though they might not support the zooming effect, 50mm is good for taking portraits. This will even produce a good blurred image compared to lenses which support zooming.

Chapter 6: Brightening Day-time portraits

Taking portraits during an overcast or bright day might make them look a bit dark. The reason behind this is the fooling effect of the brightness on the camera. The camera then reduces its exposure for compensation. The background will then look good but the subject won't look nice.

The solution to this is not brightening the overall exposure. The foreground light should then be boosted using your flash. Setting the flash to go off is the trick behind all this since the foreground will be boosted and the subject will look perfect.

Steps

If you need to shoot portraits with a fill-in flash, do the following:

Set the mode dial of your camera to "P". The camera will then be in Program mode.

You can then pop-up the built-in flash for your camera. On some camera models, this can be achieved by pressing a button with a lightening symbol. Other allow this to be done only manually by lifting the flash open. If you find a problem in doing this, just check the manual of your camera.

You can then shoot the photos normally. The light from the background and the flash will be balanced automatically by the camera.

It is possible for the subject to be too bright. This can be solved by setting the compensation of the camera to a negative number. You can also move a little back and all will be well.

Once you are finished, the flash can then be pushed down. This is for protection purposes. The mode dial of the camera can then be switched to Auto mode.

It is worth to note that built-in flashes will only take effect for a short range of time and they are not much powerful. An external flashgun is recommended for you to reach further. Modern ones are fully automatic but these are much powerful compared to the built-in ones.

Chapter 7: Portrait Photography mistakes to avoid

Most of the portraits taken by portraits don't look like real portraits. This is due mistakes made while taking the portraits. The following are some of these mistakes and how to avoid them:

Eyes not taken sharp- a portrait image should have sharp eyes. While using a shallow depth of field, the focus should be on the yes rather than the nose and other parts of the subject. This time, you need to manually set the autofocus point for your camera rather than letting it be set automatically for you.

Consult from the camera's manual on how to do this. If the subject is not in motion, focusing can be done manually. Place the image on a tripod stand and use the live view mode. The eyes should be magnified and focused on.

Shooting widely- be keen when using wide-angle lens. When you shoot closely with wide-angle lens, the subject will appear bigger than when you do it while further. The resulting photo might look awkward since the eyes can be small, the nose can be big and the whole face can be small. The chin will look receding. The photo will definitely look awkward.

To solve this, stand further from the subject and use longer lens. The facial features will be kept in good size and proportionate. A focal length of 50mm is highly recommended. However, if you are not close to the subject, a focal length of between 70-85mm is highly recommended for a good shoulders and head shot.

When you use longer lens, the depth of field is also restricted. The resulting effect will be a blurred background but the subject will be well focused. With longer telephoto lenses, a more working space will be needed since you will be focused to stand far away from the subject to shoot a nice portrait. If you adhere to all the above, your portrait will look not only good to you but also to the other viewers.

Much Depth of field- with portraits, never use a small aperture for creation of a larger depth of field. This is because if the background is more cluttered, it will distract the subject. Use a wider aperture such as f/5.6. This technique should be employed always so that the subject will be separated from the background. In case the background is not blurred as you wished to be, the subject can be positioned a bit away from the subject. Longer depth of field is also recommended.

Unusual background- be keen on what is on the background of the subject while taking portraits. Avoid places with trees, posts and other distracting structures. Once these top on one's head, they will interfere with how the portrait looks. However, use a wide aperture to blur the background.

Use of a shallow depth of field- this might lead to a portrait with sharp eyes but the ears will be soft. This applies when you use a wide lens of about 85mm f/1.8. If you use this kind of lens, be keen on focusing. You might be forced to close the aperture for some time for you to get a sharp image. You should check the depth of field and the focus of an image by making it large on the camera's screen.

Standing at the wrong height- the kind of portrait that you get is greatly affected by the height of where you are standing relative to the subject. Always, make sure to focus on the eyes and this is why you should be at the eye-level of the subject. If the subject includes a child or children, you will then have to either lie or kneel down. Shooting below the level of the eyes of the subject can lead to a double chin in the image.

Harsh shadows- the impact of shadows on your portrait needs to be reduced by softening the light. If the sunlight is strong, identify a shady place and position the subject there. You can also to place a diffuser over the subject so as to soften the light. An off-camera flashgun can also be used to eject a burst of flash. This will boost the photo by filling shadows.

Redeye effect- this is caused by the use of flash in your camera. The closeness between the light and the lens causes light to be bounced back on the retina of the subject and then to the camera. The result will be the redeye effect. However, use of anti-redeye flash settings helps in solving this problem.

Many details- the main aim while shooting portraits is to focus on the eyes. Natural and neutral color settings are recommended when shooting JPEG images. The saturation of the skin should be kept down since pimples on the face of the subject might become much visible. It is god to shoot raw files. The skin should be unsharpened. Sharpening should only be applied to the hair and the eyes of the subject.

Chapter 8: Shooting Atmospheric portraits

To shoot atmospheric portraits, follow the following steps:

Set the camera for dark- manual mode is highly recommended for this. The next thing is to adjust the shutter speed. Set it to lower than 1/250 sec. You will have synced it with the flash. Set it fast than 1/100 sec and will be able to shoot while holding it on your hand. The ISO can be set to 800. The aperture can also be set to one stop and under correct exposure for you to darken the background.

Increase the light- commander mode is highly recommended for this. It makes it possible to trigger the flashguns and adjust how strong they are. This can be set by going to Custom settings menu and then choosing "Flash Ctrl for built-in flash". However, some cameras don't have this. You can use the built-in flash or a trigger. The flashes can then be set to Remote SU4 mode.

Form some shadows- switch the flashguns to Remote. Each of these should then be assigned to a different group. Via commander mode, switch the mode to manual (M). The flash which has been set to Group A should then be placed behind the model while the one set to Group N to the side. You can then shoot for a test. If you are not comfortable with what you get, adjust the strength of the flash until when you are okay with the light.

Get shooting- now that the exposure and flash settings are okay, you can start shooting. The main focus point on the mask of the model should also be sharp. Shoot at different poses and check the best one. The sensors of your flashgun should also be directly lined with your camera. When ready to fire, the flashguns will blink red.

If you find your flash too harsh, a diffuser can be placed in front of it so as to spread and soften the light. Assistance from someone else might need for this purpose.

You can also choose to hire costumes from dress shops. University fashion students and Local theatre groups can assist if something much good is needed.

Chapter 9: Using Flash to eliminate Harsh Shadows

When shooting portraits, harsh shadows in the background are always experienced. The following are the techniques to be employed if you need to avoid shadows in your image:

Be keen on your distance- the subject should be positioned at least 2-feet from the background. This applies even when you have used a bounced flash since it will struggle to have photos without shadows in the background.

Bounce the light- the head of the flashgun should be pointed vertically and the light should be bounced off the ceiling. This will help in avoiding subject shadows. After the light has hit the ceiling, it will be diffused and bounced around the room. The space between the background and the subject will then be illuminated.

Adjust the power and zoom- some power will be lost due to the reflection of light off the ceiling. The camera should be left to look after the exposure and the flash power should be kept at the TTL setting (standard) without compensation. To make the light spread effectively, the flash zoom should be set to 50mm.

Chapter 10: How to Hold the Camera

You need to hold the camera in the right manner so as to get a sharp portrait. This is why you do some practice on the same before starting to shoot portraits. You might have been used to the normal cameras, so learning how to hold a DSLR camera might be difficulty for you. To shoot sharp portraits, hold the camera as explained below:

Hold the camera with your right hand. The index finger should be placed over the shutter release. Ensure that you can freely press the button without the need to reposition the grip.

The lens should be rested on the left hand. It should be easy to twist the lens's barrel with the hands for the purpose of zooming or focusing. The right hand should be in a position to grip the body of the camera.

The elbows should be tucked into the body. The camera will be sturdy.

While shooting a portrait, the camera needs to be switched to portrait orientation. You should then turn it so that the shutter release will be seated at the top.

The camera should be placed to the eye with the viewfinder rested against the eyebrow. This will ensure more stability.

To remain balanced, place your legs spread apart. One leg should be moved forward if you have leaned.

When taking a shot, breathe out. Breathing in or holding the breath will make you move, and the resulting portrait will look fuzzy.

A mart is good if you are kneeling while taking portraits outdoors. This is because you might find a wet place, thus, you will not be comfortable while taking the shots.

Get down into a crouching position and then bring your leg up. You will have formed a human tripod. Place the elbow on the knee. This will make you connect both the leg and the arm together. You will then remain stable while taking the shots.

The hands should be placed in such a way that the thumb can access all the controls located at the back of the camera. This is for purpose of adjusting the shooting settings.

You can also place a level surface such as a table at your front and rest your elbows on it. Remember to kneel down to be on the eye-level of the subject. This will make you steadier.

If you don't have a tripod stand and you want to shoot at a low shutter speed, lean against a wall. This will greatly support your camera.

Conclusion

It can be concluded that portrait photography involves taking photos of an individual(s) for the purpose of expressing their moods, expression or personality. Portraits can be taken using a DSLR camera which is a digital camera. One can also show the body of the individual(s) in the photo but this is not a must.

One needs to understand the various settings of the DSLR camera while taking portraits. Note that there are different kinds of portraits but almost the same settings for the camera are needed. What will differ are the techniques to be utilized.

One also needs to check on the position of the subject relative to himself and the background. For instance, objects such as trees, posts and some other structures are distracting, so avoid these when shooting portraits. The background is also not of importance in portraits. This is why most portrait photographers choose to blur it.

It is also good to make sure that the camera is help at a level which is the same as the eyes of the subject. This might force you to kneel. A mart is good when forced to kneel outdoors as you will feel much comfortable.

However, don't be too sharp on the skin of the subject as this might not be good for individuals who are old or the ones with pimples on their face. For portraits, you are only required to be sharp on the hair and the eyes.

A steady camera is good for one to shoot a nice portrait. To achieve this, a tripod stand is good. You can also identify somewhere where you can place your arms such as a table or any other flat surface. You can also lean against a wall. One also needs to understand how to set the aperture so as to get an amazing portrait.

www.ingramcontent.com/pod-product-compliance
Lightning Source LLC
Chambersburg PA
CBHW070224210526
45169CB00024B/1537

* 9 7 8 1 5 3 5 1 6 3 7 5 0 *